D0591305

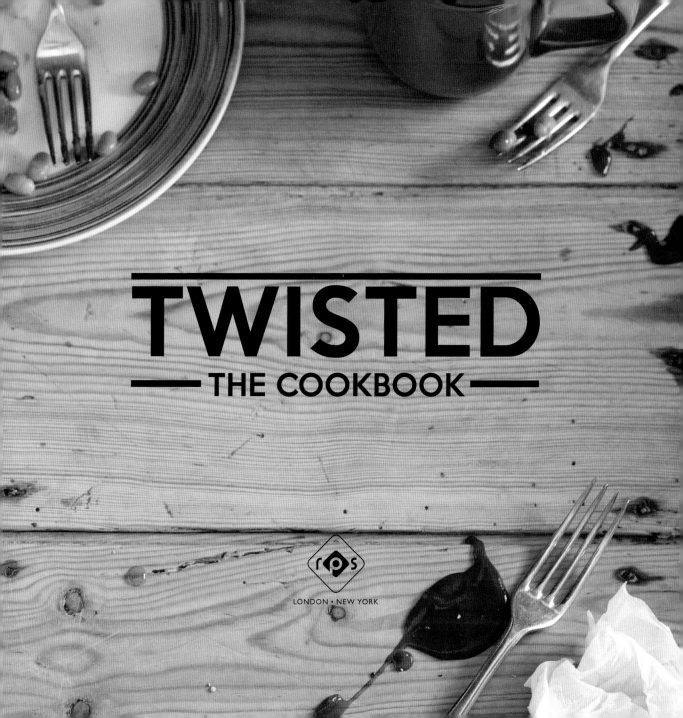

TWISTED

— THE COOKBOOK —

LONDON · NEW YORK

Art director: Sally Powell
Editor: Gillian Haslam
Production manager: Gordana Simakovic
Publisher: Cindy Richards

Photographer: Stephen Conroy
Chef: Tom Jackson
Chef's assistant: Lydia McKee
Food stylist: Kim Sullivan

First published in 2016 by Ryland Peters & Small
20–21 Jockey's Fields   341 E 116th St
London WC1R 4BW   New York, NY 10029

www.rylandpeters.com

10 9 8 7 6 5 4 3

Text © Team Twisted 2016
Design and photography © Ryland Peters & Small 2016

ISBN: 978 1 84975 844 4

A CIP catalog record for this book is available from
the Library of Congress and the British Library.

Printed in Slovenia

CONTENTS

INTRODUCTION

Having a meal with others is something we do a hell of a lot. It's also, we believe, one of the most underrated, underestimated, and misunderstood rituals in life. We take it for granted. We must eat to survive, sure, but this fact breeds complacency. Too often we retire from dinner brow-beaten from heated conversation and lumpy mashed potato. Every time you get round the table, or plonk yourself down in front of the game with pals, you should be smiling, but that's often easier said than done.

We know the feeling: you've flicked through every cookbook and food channel going, but you still don't know what to make for dinner. Your tastebuds are calling out for something new, a little bit naughty, and quite possibly wrapped in bacon.

Don't despair, because the following recipes are guaranteed to kick your kitchen into gear with some of the simplest, tastiest, and most twisted food combinations you've ever seen. If you make any of the recipes that follow in this little book, you'll be sure to make a few people smile. They might even laugh at what you've made. But we can almost guarantee they'll wash the dishes *and* they'll be back tomorrow.

Don't just take our word for it—Twisted's recipes have been rescuing millions of hungry viewers from the dull dinner apocalypse, adding a daily dash of food porn to newsfeeds all over the world. We want to show you our take on some of the most beloved comfort food from across the planet. Our recipes have been viewed more than one billion million times on Facebook and many of our most-loved and biggest viewed dishes are featured in this book. But that's just the half of it. The rest? That's just for you.

When you're hankering after a meal that's a trifle strange, offbeat, or downright weird, look no further than Twisted.

BREAKFAST

Breakfast is the most important meal of the day, right? Go big, or go home. You're probably already at home, and probably hungover. So go big! Here we have prepared for you a completely mind-bending hybrid feast inspired by two much-loved classics. The Great British Fry Up and a platter of American nachos—when combined, these are 10000% greater than the sum of their parts. Seriously, try them.

SERVES 4
HOW EASY? WITH EYES CLOSED

BREAKFAST NACHOS

1 loaf of sliced white bread

unsalted butter

12 sausages

16 slices of streaky bacon

4 eggs

3 portobello mushrooms

oil, for frying

1 can baked beans in tomato sauce

tomato ketchup

1 Preheat the oven to 200°C/400°F/Gas 6.

2 Cut the crusts off the slices of bread, then cut each slice diagonally into rough triangles. Butter each triangle, pop on a couple of baking trays, and bake for 10 minutes in the preheated oven.

3 Meanwhile, cook all the breakfast items. Broil/grill or fry the sausages and bacon, fry the eggs, slice and fry the mushrooms, heat the beans—you know the drill!

4 Remove the "nachos" from the oven. Drain on paper towels, then arrange on a large serving tray or platter, as you would tortilla chips. Pile on all the other breakfast items—sausages, bacon, mushrooms, beans, eggs, and a good squeeze of ketchup. Enjoy!

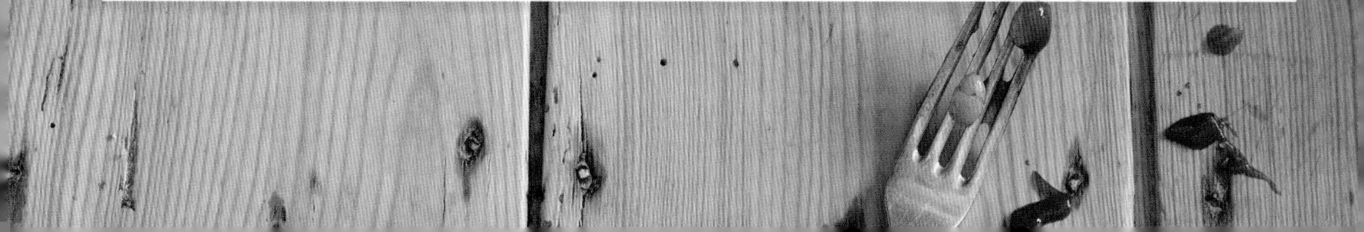

9 slices of thick, unsmoked streaky bacon

oil, for greasing and frying

6 eggs

1 crusty sourdough baguette, cut into 3 sandwich-sized lengths

salted butter, softened

3½ oz/100g liver pâté (duck is best, but chicken is also legit)

a few tablespoons of good-quality mayonnaise

a few shakes of Maggi seasoning (soy sauce is also fine)

1 hot red chili, sliced

a good few sprigs of cilantro/coriander

FOR THE PICKLES:

⅔ cup/150ml rice wine vinegar

½ cup/100g sugar, and to taste

½ tablespoon coriander seeds

a good pinch of salt

1 inch/2.5cm piece of cinnamon stick

1 cup/235ml water

1 daikon radish, cut into matchsticks

1 carrot, cut into matchsticks

1 cucumber, cut into thin, long slices

FOR THE SPICE MIX:

1 inch/2.5cm piece of cinnamon stick

1 tablespoon fennel seeds

2 cloves

1 star anise

½ tablespoon black peppercorns

Next to Pho, Bánh mì are up there with the best of Vietnamese street food. You may already know this. What you may not know, however, is that these inspired sandwiches can now be a big part of your weekend breakfast ritual. It already is here at Twisted. Everyone can get their hands on bacon and eggs, for goodness' sake. There is literally no excuse not to try this. Also, I'll tell you a secret—it's one of the tastiest recipes in here. From Mi to you.

BREAKFAST BÁNH MÌ

1 Make your pickles. Place the vinegar, sugar, coriander seeds, salt, and cinnamon stick in a pan and bring up to a simmer to dissolve the sugar. Leave to sit for 30 minutes (to steep and also to cool). Strain the pickling juice into a container and top up with the water. Drop in the vegetables, cover, and refrigerate. You can use the pickles straight away, but they are best after a day or so.

2 For the spice mix, toast all of your spices together until they just begin to smoke, then transfer to a pestle and mortar or grinder, and grind to a rough powder.

3 Oil your bacon slices, then sprinkle liberally with the spice mix. Cook in a hot griddle pan, flipping halfway. You want them charred in places, but not too crispy.

4 Fry your eggs in plenty of oil, sprinkling some salt and a little more of the spicing over them as you go.

5 Pop your baguette pieces briefly in a warmed oven to ensure crustiness. Rip apart down one side.

6 Spread the top side of your sandwich with butter and the bottom liberally with pâté and mayonnaise. Shake over some Maggi seasoning. Lay in your spiced bacon and fried eggs. Dress with red chili, lots of pickles, and cilantro/coriander. Oh, and get stuck in.

SERVES   4
HOW EASY?   PAINLESS

2 ripe haas avocados, stoned
 and peeled

1 scallion/spring onion, finely
 sliced

½ deseeded red chili, finely sliced

juice of ½ lime

2 tablespoons roughly chopped
 cilantro/coriander

salt

4 cooking chorizo sausages

3 tablespoons honey

8 eggs

4 English muffins, halved

½ cup/50g feta cheese, crumbled
 (optional)

a few pinches of cayenne

FOR THE SAUCE:

1½ cups/300ml Greek yogurt

3 tablespoons chipotle chilies in
 adobo (or sriracha)

juice of ½ lime

pinch of salt

In 1894, a hungover Lemuel Benedict called room service at the Waldorf, New York, and ordered toast, bacon, and two poached eggs smothered in hollandaise sauce. The Waldorf's chef was so impressed that he put the dish on his menu, and the rest is history. Of course, there are some who would say you should never mess with a classic. Those dudes are idiots. We love chorizo, avocado, and stuff. Spice is great for a hangover, too. Old Lemuel would have ordered our version, for sure.

EGGS BENEDICTO

1 Make your sauce by mixing all ingredients together in a bowl. You want it to be hollandaise sauce-consistency, so add more lime juice to thin out if necessary. Leave at room temperature.

2 Roughly mash your avocado flesh with the scallion/spring onion, chili, lime, cilantro/coriander, and a good pinch of salt. Set aside, covered.

3 Make a shallow incision down one side of your cooking chorizo. Dig your fingers in and rip open—this will give you a nice rough texture for frying. Make a couple of slashes on the other side (to stop them from curling up). Fry, ripped side down, in a hot pan for about 3 minutes until you start to get some charring. Flip and cook on the other side. Squeeze in your honey and glaze your chorizo. Remove from the heat.

4 Poach your eggs.

5 Toast your muffin halves. Spread some avocado over each half. Top with your glazed chorizo, then the poached egg. Add a couple of spoonfuls of the sauce. Crumble over some feta (if using) and fleck over some cayenne. Come on!

Here we go. Two is better than one, etc, blah blah, we get it. These guys may look familiar, but those flavor combos are not. They are also not yet on sale in any fast food chain. Fortunately for you, you can make them chez toi. These are seriously delicious.

SERVES   4
HOW EASY?   PAINLESS

DOUBLE DOWN BREAKFAST MUFFINS

10½ oz/300g baby plum tomatoes

salt

1 teaspoon sugar

¾ cup/200ml light olive oil or vegetable oil, plus extra for cooking

2 egg yolks

1 tablespoon red wine vinegar

14 oz/400g sausage meat

4 English muffins

butter, for spreading

4 eggs

8 Cheddar cheese slices

1 Preheat the oven to 200°C/400°F/Gas 6.

2 Pop your tomatoes in a roasting tray with a good pinch of salt, the sugar, and a lug of oil. Roast in the preheated oven for 30 minutes, or until starting to blister. Bring out and leave to cool.

3 Pop three-quarters of the tomatoes in the bowl of a food processor along with the egg yolks, a pinch of salt, and the vinegar. Save the other roasted tomatoes for your sandwiches. Tilt your processor to the side and start the motor. Trickle your oil in through the funnel, very slowly at first, then a little more confidently. It should catch the blade, begin to emulsify, and become mayonnaise. Once you have added all the oil, turn off the motor and taste for seasoning. If it's a little too thick, add a few more drops of vinegar or a little water to loosen. Set aside.

4 Grab a golf ball-sized piece of sausage meat. Place between two sheets of wax/greaseproof paper and flatten with your hand. The patty should be about ¼ inch/5mm thick. Repeat until you have eight of these in total. Remove the top layer of paper. Slap the sheet of the patties (meat side down) into a hot, oiled pan and remove the second layer of paper. Cook for 1 minute, then flip. You're looking for a bit of color on both sides and for the meat to be cooked through. Repeat until all of your patties are cooked.

5 Carefully slice each of your muffins into three disks of even thickness and pop under a hot broiler/grill to toast slightly. Butter the slices.

6 Fry the eggs, then layer your breakfast muffins. Bottom piece of muffin, cheese, sausage patty, middle piece of muffin, cheese, patty, tomato mayonnaise, fried egg, a few roasted tomatoes, top piece of muffin. Serve with extra mayo on the table. Legit.

Sometimes, you want a light, refreshing breakfast of oats and berries, and sometimes, you want a soft-boiled egg, placed inside an avocado, wrapped in a blanket of bacon. One might justify making our recipe by reminding themselves that avocado is the good kind of fat. As for the bacon, well you can't win 'em all... Prepare to pig out.

BACON AVOCADO EGGS

SERVES 4
HOW EASY? PAINLESS

medium eggs (1 egg for each avocado)

large, just ripe avocados

slices of smoked streaky bacon (about 8 slices for each avocado)

sunflower oil, for pan frying

1 Drop your eggs into a pan of simmering water and cook for exactly 6 minutes. Carefully lift out and place in a bowl of iced water to cool. Peel your eggs and set aside.

2 Cut your avocados in half and remove the skin in one fell swoop. Take out the stone using a knife. Further scoop out the cavity so it will snugly fit your egg. Pop your egg in and place the other half of the avocado over the egg.

3 Stretch the individual slices of bacon with the back of a knife—this will reduce shrinkage. Lay them next to each other, slightly overlapping, on a chopping board.

4 Roll your re-sealed avocado in the row of bacon slices—the row should be as wide as your avocado. Wrap two more slices around the avocado in the opposite direction to seal the avocado entirely.

5 Heat some oil in a skillet/frying pan. Fry the parcels in the pan for 10 minutes or so, turning constantly. Make sure to begin the frying with the loose ends of the bacon facing down as this will fix them in place. Get stuck in!

PARTY

For such a simple dish, there are many theories about the best way to cook/eat burgers. The debate will likely rage on until 2 + 2 = 5, but we're pretty sure we've just settled it.

SERVES 6
HOW EASY? WITH EYES CLOSED

BUFFALO CHICKEN PARTY BUNS

1 cup/130g all-purpose/plain flour

1 tablespoon paprika

1 teaspoon garlic powder

1 tablespoon cayenne

1 tablespoon salt

3 boneless, skinless chicken breasts, butterflied and cut into two

2 cups/475ml buttermilk

sunflower oil, for roasting

6 brioche burger buns

12 slices of Cheddar cheese

12 slices of streaky bacon, cooked and crispy

gherkin slices

¼ cup/60g unsalted butter

3 tablespoons honey

⅓ cup/100ml hot sauce

1 tablespoon sesame seeds

blue cheese dip, to serve

1 Preheat the oven to 220°C/425°F/Gas 7.

2 Season your flour with the paprika, garlic powder, cayenne, and salt. Drop each of your chicken pieces into the flour, dunk in the buttermilk, then throw back into the flour. Pop them all on a lined baking sheet, add a good few lugs of sunflower oil, and bake in the preheated oven for 20 minutes. (You can also deep-fry the chicken if you wish.)

3 Turn the oven temperature down to 190°C/375°F/Gas 5.

4 Cut your buns in half and place the bottom half of each in a baking tray just big enough to hold all six snugly. Lay down half of your cheese.

5 Place a piece of cooked chicken on top of each cheese slice. Top with two slices of bacon, another layer of cheese, and then a couple of gherkin slices per bun. Finish with the top bun.

6 Heat the butter, honey, and hot sauce together in a pan until bubbling. Pop in the sesame seeds and mix. Remove from the heat and pour all over the burgers.

7 Cover with foil and bake for 15 minutes, then serve with a blue cheese dip.

It would probably take you 15 minutes to get to the drive-thru, but in that time you could have a dozen of these on the table. No-brainer, right? Your guests (if they get there in time—they're that quick to make) will be swooning. The secret to this meat-lover's dream is a muffin pan. Yes, a muffin pan. The secret's out! Don't hesitate!

CHEESEBURGER MUFFINS

MAKES 12
HOW EASY? WITH EYES CLOSED

1 lb 2 oz/500g ground/minced beef

1 small white onion, diced (save a little for the topping)

1 tablespoon olive oil, plus extra for brushing

1 teaspoon salt

1 teaspoon freshly ground black pepper

1 garlic clove, finely chopped

6 brioche burger buns

12 slices of red Leicester cheese, cut into small and large pieces

tomato ketchup

mustard

gherkins, diced

1 Preheat the oven to 175°C/350°F/Gas 4.

2 Fry the beef and onion in the oil in a skillet/frying pan until nicely colored and the onion is translucent. Season well with salt and pepper, then add the garlic. Fry for a moment longer to cook the garlic. Drain the fat from the pan and set aside.

3 Slice your burger buns in half, then place each half in a muffin tray, cut side facing upward. Push into the tray to form a cup, then brush with oil.

4 Place a small square of cheese in each burger bun cup. Divide your burger mixture between the cups, filling them well. Top with another slightly larger square of cheese. Bake in the preheated oven for 10 minutes.

5 Top with ketchup, mustard, gherkin, and onion. Get involved!

Squid often struggles to assert itself on a menu. Calamari, however? A best-seller. Apparently if you dust things with breadcrumbs and deep-fry them, they become 150% more appealing—even slimy sea creatures! Weird, huh? Here we've tossed the final product in some buttery hot sauce for that buffalo-wing tang. Enjoy!

SERVES 4
HOW EASY? WITH EYES CLOSED

BUFFALO FRIED CALAMARI

1¼ cups/300ml buttermilk

½ tablespoon smoked sweet paprika

½ tablespoon cayenne

1 tablespoon salt

14 oz/400g fresh squid rings

1½ cups/200g all-purpose/plain flour

sunflower oil, for deep-frying

3½ tablespoons/50g butter

3½ tablespoons hot sauce

FOR THE RANCH DRESSING:

1½ tablespoons roughly chopped fresh dill

½ tablespoon fresh oregano leaves

½ tablespoon finely chopped fresh chives

1 cup/215g soured cream

1 cup/225g mayonnaise

juice of ½ lemon

½ garlic clove, crushed to a paste

½ teaspoon freshly ground black pepper

salt

1 Season the buttermilk with the paprika, cayenne, and salt. Pop in the squid rings and leave to marinate for an hour or so in the fridge.

2 Mix together all the dressing ingredients and set aside.

3 Remove the squid using a slotted spoon (allow the excess buttermilk to drain away) and drop into the flour, to which you have added a little salt. Shake around in the bowl, using your fingers to toss occasionally (you may need to do this in batches). Remove from the flour. Repeat with all of the rings. Deep-fry in the sunflower oil for about 1 minute until nicely golden. Drain briefly on kitchen paper and tip into a serving dish.

4 Melt the butter and hot sauce together in a small pan, then pour over the fried squid rings. Toss to coat, then serve with the ranch dressing.

Look at these little guys! Good old potatoes. They're usually pretty good as they are, to be fair, all softly baked and smeared with salty butter. But come on, seriously, we're Twisted. We love to wrap and stuff things. It's what we do. Here we do both, and the end product tastes completely brilliant. Etna, Vesuvius, that one in Iceland that grounded all the planes a few years ago? These are far more impressive. Make your own and watch out for the lava!

SERVES 4
HOW EASY? WITH EYES CLOSED

ERUPTING POTATO VOLCANOES

1 packet of baby potatoes

smoked streaky bacon (1 slice for each potato)

vegetable oil, for brushing

sticky barbecue sauce, for glazing

red Leicester (or Cheddar) cheese, cut into fat sticks 1 inch/2.5cm long

1 Preheat the oven to 200°C/400°F/Gas 6. Line a baking tray with baking parchment.

2 Parboil your potatoes in a pan of salted water for 5 minutes. Drain and cool slightly.

3 Slice off one end of each potato so that they can stand up. Wrap a slice of bacon as tightly as possible around each potato, leaving a small opening at the top. Pin the bacon a couple of times using toothpicks—this will prevent unfurling. Hollow out the top of the potato—you will stuff this with cheese later.

4 Place your potatoes on the lined baking tray. Brush with oil and bake in the preheated oven for 30 minutes, or until the bacon is starting to crisp. Bring out, remove the toothpicks, and glaze the bacon with barbecue sauce. Pop back in the oven for another 10 minutes.

5 When you are ready to serve, place a stick of cheese in each of the cavities you created earlier. A few more minutes in the oven, and your volcanoes are erupting!

There's more to Tokyo than anime, hair dye, and robotic vending machines. Like some kind of delicious disaster movie, this urban jungle is awash with flavor. From Michelin-starred rooftop restaurants to the smoky labyrinth of street vendors, you can taste your way around the city one bite at a time. Unfortunately, flights are expensive. So we've taken the tastes of Tokyo, twisted in a bit of Korea, and created something incredible. "World's tastiest triangles" is a bit of a weird accolade. But we've certainly managed it.

SERVES 4
HOW EASY? SWEATING A BIT

TOKYO SANDWICHES

2 cups/375g sushi rice

1 tablespoon sugar

1 teaspoon salt

¼ cup/60ml rice vinegar

4 nori seaweed sheets

1 small carrot, finely shredded

½ cup/25g cooked spinach, squeezed to remove excess moisture

1 fried egg

2 tablespoons gochujang chili paste, mixed with ½ cup/100g mayonnaise

FOR THE BEEF BULGOGI SANDWICH:

1 thick sirloin steak, about 7 oz/200g

4 garlic cloves, finely chopped

1 teaspoon finely chopped ginger

2 scallions/spring onions, chopped

2 tablespoons soy sauce

2 tablespoons brown sugar

½ teaspoon freshly ground black pepper

1 tablespoon toasted sesame oil

FOR THE KATSU SANDWICH:

1 boneless, skinless chicken breast, butterflied

⅓ cup/50g all-purpose/plain flour

1 egg, beaten

2 cups/100g panko breadcrumbs

oil, for frying

white cabbage, finely shredded

½ teaspoon salt, plus extra for seasoning

2 tablespoons mayonnaise

1 tablespoon rice vinegar

1 scallion/spring onion, finely shredded

tonkatsu sauce (brown or steak sauce will do)

FOR THE SANDWICHES:

1 Cook your sushi rice according to the packet instructions, then drain and leave to cool almost completely. In a small saucepan, dissolve the sugar and salt into the rice vinegar. Remove from the heat, cool slightly, then stir through the still warm, cooked rice.

2 Cut your nori sheets down to sandwich-sized squares. Spread a thin layer of rice onto one side of each square. Now for your fillings (but note that the beef needs time to marinate).

FOR THE BEEF BULGOGI:

3 Make your bulgogi marinade by mixing everything except the steak together in a bowl. Slice your steak as thinly as possible and add to the marinade. Pop in the fridge for a couple of hours (or longer if possible).

4 When ready to cook, fry off your beef, along with your marinade, in a hot pan until starting to color and cooked through.

5 Add some shredded carrot and spinach to a rice/nori square. Place down your beef. Add your fried egg and a few spoonfuls of the gochujang mayonnaise. Place another rice square on top, flatten, and slice.

FOR THE KATSU:

6 Bash your chicken breast to a $^3/_8$ inch/9mm thickness. Season well with salt. Coat in flour, then egg, then panko breadcrumbs. Shallow-fry in hot oil until nicely dark and crispy, and the chicken is cooked through. Set aside on some kitchen paper.

7 Mix the shredded cabbage with the salt, mayonnaise, and rice vinegar. Add some dressed cabbage to one rice/nori square. Add some scallion/spring onion. Lay the chicken on top. Dress with tonkatsu sauce. Top with another rice square (rice facing down). Flatten with your hand and cut into neat triangles.

There's no denying that hosting a party full of hungry friends is a tricky business. Just putting it out there: if all you're going to serve at your shindig is hummus, carrots, and cocktail sausages, no one will want to be your friend. On the other hand, whipping out this glistening, oozing tray of cheeseburger-y joy is a surefire way to turn your guests' frowns upside down. The whole thing can be prepared beforehand. The ultimate game-day food solution.

SERVES 6
HOW EASY? WITH EYES CLOSED

CHEESEBURGER PARTY BUNS

1 lb 10 oz/750g ground/minced beef

salt and freshly ground black pepper

6 brioche burger buns

12 slices of red Leicester cheese

6 slices of streaky bacon, cooked until crispy and cut in half

12 gherkin slices

1/3 cup/75g unsalted butter

2 tablespoons brown sugar

4 tablespoons tomato ketchup

4 tablespoons mustard

4 tablespoons Worcestershire sauce

1 tablespoon sesame seeds

1 Preheat the oven to 190°C/375°F/Gas 5.

2 Brown your mince in a skillet/frying pan and season with salt and pepper. Drain off any fat from the pan and set aside.

3 Cut your buns in half and place the bottom half of each in a baking tray just big enough to hold all six snugly. Lay down half of your cheese.

4 Cover the bun halves with all the mince. Add two slices of cheese to each bun, then add the crispy bacon and gherkin slices. Top with the other bun halves.

5 Mix together the butter, sugar, ketchup, mustard, and Worcestershire sauce in a small pan over a medium heat. Add the sesame seeds, stir to combine, then remove from the heat and pour over the burgers.

6 Cover with foil and bake in the preheated oven for 15 minutes.

4 boneless, skinless chicken thighs

sunflower oil, for shallow-frying the chicken

8 thick slices of sourdough bread

butter, for frying the sandwiches

FOR THE MARINADE:

2 cups/500ml buttermilk

juice of 1 lemon

1 tablespoon salt

2 bay leaves, slightly crushed

FOR THE DREDGE:

2¼ cups/300g all-purpose/plain flour

1 tablespoon fine salt

½ tablespoon dried or fresh oregano

½ tablespoon mixed dried sweet herbs (marjoram, basil, sage)

1 teaspoon cayenne

1 teaspoon freshly ground black pepper

FOR THE CHEESE PASTE:

10½ oz/300g Comté or Gruyère cheese

1 tablespoon freshly chopped tarragon

4 tablespoons heavy/double cream

2 egg yolks

½ garlic clove, crushed to a paste

1 heaped teaspoon Dijon mustard

A grilled cheese sandwich is one of those dishes that will go down in history as a complete and utter classic. And what does Twisted like to do to the classics? Completely turn them on their heads, that's what. Fried chicken and a grilled cheese sandwich? This is a twist not to be sniffed at. Although admittedly, it'll be pretty hard not to sniff once these smells start to permeate your kitchen.

FRIED CHICKEN MELTS

1 Mix together the ingredients for the buttermilk marinade. Bash your chicken thighs nice and thin. Drop into your marinade and leave in the fridge for a few hours.

2 Season your flour with the salt, herbs, cayenne, and pepper. Allow the marinade to drip off the chicken pieces, then dredge the chicken in the flour. Toss gently—the craggy bits are what you want.

3 Shallow-fry the coated chicken in hot oil for 6–8 minutes, flipping halfway. Remove and drain on kitchen towel. Ensure the chicken is cooked all the way through. Repeat with the other pieces.

4 Make your cheese paste. Pop everything in a food processor and pulse until you have a spreadable mixture. Add a little more cream if the consistency isn't quite right.

5 Grab two slices of bread. Spread both with the paste. Lay your fried chicken piece down on one cheese-laden slice, then top with the other (cheese side down) to complete the sandwich.

6 Melt some butter in a skillet/frying pan and place over a medium heat. Lay in your chicken sandwiches, two at a time if enough room, and fry. Flip after 3–4 minutes and fry the other side. They should be deeply golden, crunchy, and the cheese should be oozing through the gaps in the bread. Serious.

Like happiness, love, and contentment, no one is sure of the origin of the donut. Yet it's a cornerstone of the proverbial bakery aisle. Weird, huh? You ask a three-year-old what their favorite food is and they'll probably say something like, "A donut, obviously, you idiot." Until now you couldn't eat donuts for every meal. Well, we made it our mission to appease this hypothetical toddler and the other donut lovers out there, and created the dinner donut. Mind blow-nut.

MAKES ABOUT 10
HOW EASY? PAINLESS

¼ cup/60ml tomato sauce

¼ cup/60g ricotta

1 ball of mozzarella, torn into small pieces

a bunch of small basil leaves

1 red chili, finely sliced

sunflower oil, for shallow-frying

grated Parmesan cheese, to serve

FOR THE DOUGH:

4½ cups/600g strong bread flour, plus extra for dusting

1½ tablespoons sugar

1 tablespoon fine salt

1½ cups/350ml lukewarm water

2 teaspoons instant yeast

2 tablespoons olive oil, plus a little extra for greasing the bowl

PIZZA "DONUTS"

1 To make the dough, pop your flour in the bowl of a food processor. Add the sugar and salt and pulse to distribute. Pour in your water, then add your yeast and oil. Start the motor. Run it for about 20 seconds—it should come together into a large, slightly sticky mass.

2 Tip the mixture out onto a floured surface and knead for 5 minutes or so until you have a pretty smooth ball. Place in an oiled bowl, rub with a little oil, cover with plastic wrap, and leave somewhere warm-ish to prove for 1 hour.

3 Push down the risen dough a little to knock some air out, then tear off a nugget-sized piece with a floured hand. Shape into a rough ball, then flatten out gently. Fill with a little tomato sauce, ricotta, mozzarella, basil, and chili.

4 Place the flat, filled "pizza" in one hand. Using the other hand, pinch up each of the sides to form a sealed ball. Place on a floured surface, pinched side facing down, then repeat to make your other "donuts."

5 Fry in a couple of inches of sunflower oil, flipping once to brown the other side. The donuts should puff up. After about 4 minutes, they should be ready. Fry in batches if necessary, and drain on kitchen towels.

6 Dust with lots of Parmesan, then get stuck in!

3 bell peppers (red, green, and
  yellow), sliced

2 red onions, sliced

1 cup/200ml passata/strained
  chopped tomatoes

⅓ cup/75ml hot sauce

4 boneless, skinless chicken breasts

1 teaspoon ground cumin

1½ teaspoons sugar

1½ teaspoons salt

1 teaspoon pepper

1 tablespoon paprika

3 garlic cloves, chopped

2 tablespoons olive oil, plus extra
  for drizzling

6 flour tortillas

FOR THE CHEESE SAUCE:

3½ tablespoons/50g butter

¼ cup/40g all-purpose/plain flour

1 cup/250ml whole milk

3 tablespoons hot sauce

2¼ cups/200g grated Red
  Leicester cheese

salt

FOR THE TOPPING:

1 large ripe tomato, diced

1 avocado, peeled, stoned,
  and diced

a few cilantro/coriander leaves

If you thought a slow cooker could only be used for funky old stews, you can think again. Packed with flavor, these incredible fajita chicken nachos make perfect use of that slow cooker that's been gathering dust in the back of your kitchen cupboard. Simply whack all the ingredients in the pot, turn it on, and return to more deliciousness than you can shake a nacho at. For all you little devils out there, please feel free to add extra hot sauce. You know you want to.

SLOW-COOKER FAJITA CHICKEN NACHOS

1 Grab your slow cooker. Chuck in the peppers, onions, passata, and hot sauce. Pop the chicken breasts on top, then season with the cumin, sugar, salt, pepper, paprika, and garlic. Pour in the olive oil, throw the lid on, set your slow cooker to high, and cook for 3½ hours.

2 Preheat the oven to 180°C/350°F/Gas 4. Using a pizza cutter, slice each of the tortillas into six fat triangular nachos. Drizzle over some oil, place on a baking tray, and bake for 10 minutes. Leave to cool, then load into a big serving dish.

3 Remove the chicken from the slow cooker, shred with forks, then return to the sauce and mix together.

4 Make your cheese sauce. Heat the butter in a pan until foaming, then add the flour. Cook off before adding the milk, little by little. Add the hot sauce, then add the cheese. Cook over a very low heat, stirring, until fully melted. Season and keep warm.

5 Spoon the saucy pulled chicken all over your nachos. Top with cheese sauce, diced tomato, avocado, and cilantro/coriander. Get stuck in!

Ok, we'll admit it. We don't like cauliflower cheese. Or at least we didn't until we tried these. Round, crispy, cheesy—all words we like. Why not, we thought, and by Jove are we happy we tried 'em. These little guys are one of the more decadent bites you'll ever taste, and are perfect as starters, shares, or snacks.

MAKES ABOUT 10
HOW EASY? PAINLESS

CAULIFLOWER CHEESE CROQUETTES

1 cauliflower, broken into large florets

3 tablespoons olive oil

2 eggs, beaten

4 cups/200g panko breadcrumbs

sunflower oil, for deep-frying

FOR THE BÉCHAMEL SAUCE:

1 small onion

4 cloves

2 cups/500ml whole milk

1 bay leaf

1/3 cup/75g unsalted butter

1/3 cup/50g all-purpose/plain flour, plus extra for dusting

a good few scrapes of nutmeg

salt and freshly ground black pepper

1 heaped teaspoon Dijon mustard

1 1/2 cups/150g grated sharp, mature Cheddar cheese

1 Cut your onion into quarters and stud each quarter with a clove. Pop your milk in a saucepan, then add the onion and bay leaf. Bring to a boil, then remove from the heat and leave to sit, covered, for 30 minutes or so. Strain.

2 Meanwhile, preheat the oven to 220°C/425°F/Gas 7.

3 Blanch your cauliflower florets in a pan of boiling water for 5 minutes or so, or until al dente. Drain and pop on a baking tray, dress with the olive oil, and roast in the preheated oven for 5 minutes to get a bit of color on them (and also to dry them out). Leave to cool, then chop roughly—a few chunks are good.

4 Make your cheesy béchamel sauce. Melt the butter in a saucepan until foaming, then add the flour. Whisk together to form a loose paste and allow to cook off for a couple of minutes over a low heat (it should smell like cookies/biscuits).

5 Add your seasoned milk little by little, whisking as you go to eradicate any lumps. Once all the milk is incorporated, allow to cook over a low heat until nicely thick. Season well with nutmeg, pepper, and salt, stir through the mustard, then add your cheese and immediately remove from the heat. Stir until the cheese has melted, then leave to cool almost completely.

6 Add your cauliflower pieces to the sauce and stir to coat. Transfer to a shallow tray, cover with plastic wrap, and pop in the freezer for 30 minutes—you want the mix to be a little springy to the touch and no longer sticky.

7 Remove from the freezer. Grab rough, golf ball-sized lumps of the mixture. Roll in your palms, then dust with flour. Repeat. Dunk each ball into beaten egg, then into breadcrumbs and set aside.

8 Deep-fry in oil preheated to 175°C/350°F for 2–3 minutes, or until deep golden brown. Drain on kitchen paper and serve.

NEXT LEVEL

Twisted are very pleased to inform you that cakes are finally cool again. No longer confined to your Great Auntie Mabel's larder, these round, layered, sweet creations have been given a makeover, sexed up, and most importantly of all, you can now eat them for dinner. That's right dudes, savory cakes are the future, and this slice of fajita-style genius should be top of your list. Make it.

SERVES 6
HOW EASY? WITH EYES CLOSED

FAJITA CAKE

3 red onions, sliced

6 bell peppers (red, yellow, orange—you decide!), sliced

5 large boneless, skinless chicken breasts

4 tablespoons olive oil

2 teaspoons salt

3 tablespoons/50g fajita seasoning

6 large flour tortillas

8 oz/235g can of black/turtle beans, drained and rinsed

1 cup/200g tomato salsa

1 cup/90g grated Cheddar cheese

1 cup/215g soured cream, for "frosting"

sprigs of cilantro/coriander and red chili, for decoration (optional)

1 Preheat the oven to 190°C/375°F/Gas 5.

2 Pop your onions, mixed peppers, and chicken down on a large baking tray. Toss in the oil, salt, and fajita seasoning. Shove in the preheated oven for 30 minutes. Bring out and leave to cool slightly.

3 Cut the chicken breasts into bite-sized pieces and set aside.

4 Line a 9½ inch/24cm springform cake pan with baking parchment. Increase the oven temperature to 200°C/400°F/Gas 6.

5 Warm your tortillas briefly by popping them one by one into a warm oven for 15 seconds. Place one in the base of the cake pan, then add a layer of peppers and onions, a layer of chicken, black beans, salsa, and cheese. Pop another tortilla on top and repeat the process until everything is used up.

6 Fold the edges of the final tortilla in on itself to create a neat lid. Cover with foil and bake for 15 minutes.

7 Uncover and leave to cool slightly, then remove from the cake pan. "Frost" the top with soured cream and decorate with cilantro/coriander and chili (if using). Marvel at your creation, then destroy.

SERVES 6
HOW EASY? PAINLESS

1 extra-large cauliflower

3½ tablespoons/50g melted butter, for glazing

FOR THE TIKKA MARINADE:

1½ cups/300ml thick Greek yogurt

½ cup/100ml heavy/double cream

2 tablespoons tomato paste/purée

2 fat garlic cloves, grated

1 inch/2.5cm piece of ginger, grated

1 long green chili, finely chopped

2 tablespoons smoked paprika

1 tablespoon chili powder

1 tablespoon ground coriander

1 teaspoon ground cumin

2 tablespoons runny honey

juice of 1 lemon

½ tablespoon fine salt

FOR THE RAITA:

2¼ cups/500ml natural yogurt

¼ cucumber, diced into
   ½ inch/1cm chunks

good pinch of salt

juice of ½ lemon

1 tablespoon finely chopped
   cilantro/coriander

1½ tablespoons finely chopped
   fresh mint

In a completely unexpected turn of events, the cauliflower has become cool again. That weird old white brain (that you honestly believed grew on the moon until recently) has been given a new lease of life, and is being used in recipes all over the net in place of rice, pizza, and even grilled cheese. Fair play to the guy, he scrubs up pretty well. This particular recipe takes good old Coli-n to India. He had a great time—here's one of the snaps from the trip.

WHOLE TIKKA CAULIFLOWER

1 Remove the outer leaves of the cauliflower and cut out most of the core (leaving the cauliflower intact). Blanch the whole cauliflower, with its root facing downward, in a pan of boiling, salted water for 5 minutes. Remove and leave to dry out.

2 Make your tikka marinade. Pop all of the ingredients in a food processor and blend. It wants to be fairly thick, so add more yogurt if necessary. Cover your dried cauliflower with the mixture and place in a roasting pan. Leave to marinate in the fridge for as long as you fancy—about 4 hours should do it.

3 Preheat the oven to 220°C/425°F/Gas 7.

4 Brush the cauliflower all over with the melted butter and roast in the preheated oven for 30–40 minutes, re-applying more butter from time to time.

5 Mix together the ingredients for the raita and leave to sit for 20 minutes or so before using. Get stuck in!

If you're not entirely sure what a fattee is, don't worry. Four words: flatbread covered in stuff. Traditionally, fatteh is a celebratory dish often eaten around Christmastime in Lebanon. Our kind-of Indian version is designed to be eaten all year round, at any time, day or night. Is that not a cause for celebration? Fattee time.

TWISTED'S CHICKEN FATTEE

SERVES 6–8
HOW EASY? SWEATING A BIT

FOR THE CHICKEN:
1 good-quality chicken, about
   3½ lb/1.6kg
oil, for rubbing into the chicken
2 teaspoons ground cinnamon
½ teaspoon ground cloves
1 teaspoon garam masala
1 tablespoon salt

FOR THE RICE PILAF:
3 cups/500g white basmati rice
3 onions, finely sliced in half moons
½ cup/100g unsalted butter

1 stick of cinnamon
8 green cardamom pods
8 oz/240g can of garbanzo beans/
   chickpeas, drained and rinsed
chicken stock—See step 5 for
   quantity

FOR THE FATTEE:
1 large eggplant/aubergine, diced
   into 1 inch/2.5cm chunks
salt
1 teaspoon ground cumin
sunflower oil, for frying

FOR THE SEASONED YOGURT:
1½ cups/300ml strained Greek
   yogurt
a small handful of fresh mint leaves
a small handful of cilantro/
   coriander leaves
1 teaspoon freshly grated ginger
½ garlic clove
1 green chili
1 heaped teaspoon sugar, or to
   taste
juice of ½ lemon
½ teaspoon salt

TO SERVE:
2 naan breads
Bombay mix of your choosing—
   a nutty, spicy one is good
dried rose petals
cilantro/coriander leaves
a good pinch of saffron strands,
   soaked in a little hot water for
   30 minutes (optional)
lemon wedges

1 Wash your rice under running water until the water runs clear, then leave to soak in salted, lukewarm water for an hour or so.

2 Preheat the oven to 220°C/425°F/Gas 7.

3 Place the chicken in a roasting pan and rub all over with the ground cinnamon, cloves, garam masala, and salt. Rub with oil, then roast in the preheated oven for 20 minutes. Drop the temperature to 160°C/325°F/Gas 3 and cook for about 1½ hours, basting occasionally, until you have good color and the wings slip off when pinched.

4 While the chicken is in the oven, get on with your rice base. Fry the sliced onions very slowly in the butter with the cinnamon stick and the cardamom pods. You want them to be super jammy, soft, and translucent—this will take 30–40 minutes.

5 When the onions are ready, drain your soaked rice in a sieve. Add the rice to the onion mix along with the drained garbanzo beans/chickpeas and turn the heat up a little. Using a metal spoon, gently fold the rice in the butter, trying to coat each grain with a slick of grease. When you can hear a sizzle at the bottom of the pan, pour in chicken stock until it comes ½ in/1cm above the rice. Check the liquid for seasoning. Cover with wet baking parchment and add a tight lid. Cook over a high heat for 4 minutes, then turn down to low for a further 6 minutes. Turn off the heat and leave to steam for 15–20 minutes.

6 Dust your eggplant/aubergine pieces liberally with fine salt and place in a colander to drain for a good 30 minutes. Rinse with water and pat very dry with kitchen towels. Dust with the cumin and shallow-fry in hot oil until soft and golden. Set aside.

7 Brush the naan with a little butter and bake in the oven until mostly crispy and a little charred. Crack them up and place on the bottom of a large serving dish.

8 Pop all the seasoned yoghurt ingredients in a food processor and blend to the consistency of light/single cream. Loosen with a little water if too thick.

9 Check the chicken is cooked through, then remove from the oven and leave to rest for 10 minutes.

10 Tip the pilaf out on top of the baked naan. Rip the chicken into portions and place over the rice. Deglaze the chicken roasting pan with a little stock and pour this over the rice and chicken.

11 Top with the eggplant/aubergines, yoghurt sauce, Bombay mix, rose petals, and cilantro/coriander. Sprinkle over the saffron water (if using) and serve with the lemon wedges. Crush it.

Ahh, the Camembert Hedgehog Bread—a stalwart of Twisted's cheese repertoire. Trust us, this will be your next dinner party show-stopper. Even the most amateur (and possibly drunk) chef should feel right at home with this dish, but its ease is only half the appeal. All it takes is six ingredients, ten minutes to make and twenty to bake, and boom, food heaven (and lots of weird dreams to boot).

CAMEMBERT HEDGEHOG BREAD

SERVES   4
HOW EASY?   WITH EYES CLOSED

1 large, whole Camembert for baking, all packaging removed

1 large sourdough loaf (or any other large loaf of bread)

2 tablespoons finely chopped fresh rosemary, plus a few small sprigs

3 fat garlic cloves, finely chopped, plus a few slivers

6 tablespoons olive oil

sea salt flakes

1 Preheat the oven to 175°C/350°F/Gas 4.

2 Using the bottom of your Camembert box as a stencil, cut a hole in the middle of the loaf. Tear away the bread to make the hole as deep as the Camembert.

3 Working around this central cavity, carefully cut your loaf in both directions almost all the way down to the bottom of the loaf (it's important not to cut through the bottom crust). You want to have 1-inch (2.5-cm) squared individual segments (the perfect size for dunking).

4 Score one side of the Camembert and cut away the rind. Pop the cheese, cut side up, in the bread hole.

5 Mix the chopped rosemary and chopped garlic into the olive oil and spoon all over the loaf, encouraging the flavored oil into all the slits. Cover the loaf liberally with sea salt flakes. Pop a few mini sprigs of rosemary and a few garlic slivers in the middle of the cheese, along with a little drizzle of olive oil.

6 Bake in the preheated oven for 20 minutes and get your mates round.

When we first tried a Philly Cheesesteak, we received a round of applause (it's the American way). It's with this star-spangled enthusiasm that we have created a new take on the idea. Why the hell not? Drawing inspiration from Tex-Mex—a style of food which a certain blonde billionaire businessman would never approve of—Philly Cheesesteak Potato Nachos are the best of all worlds. The mix of flavors, textures, and geographical influences is sure to impress. The perfect wildcard at any dinner party or BBQ, this recipe takes the idea of a sharing plate, smashes it, and starts all over again.

SERVES   4
HOW EASY? PAINLESS

PHILLY CHEESESTEAK POTATO NACHOS

6 large baking potatoes

sunflower oil

1 tablespoon smoked paprika

2 green bell peppers, sliced

2 onions, sliced

a good few shakes of Worcestershire sauce

1 fat rib-eye steak, about 14 oz/ 400g, at room temperature

3 cups/300g grated provolone cheese

fresh oregano, to garnish

diced tomato, to garnish (optional)

salt and freshly ground black pepper

1 Preheat the oven to 200°C/400°F/Gas 6. Line some baking trays with baking parchment.

2 Peel the potatoes and slice to a ¼ inch/5mm thickness. Pop in a large bowl of water to rinse away some of the starch, then drain and pat completely dry. Coat the slices liberally in oil and place individually on the lined baking trays. Sprinkle with salt and a little paprika and bake for 30–40 minutes, flipping halfway, until nicely colored and crisp. Remove from the oven and drain on some kitchen towel. Leave the oven on.

3 Meanwhile, fry the peppers and onions in 3 tablespoons of oil over a medium/high heat, stirring frequently. You want them to be soft but also a little charred in places. When they are ready, shake in the Worcestershire sauce and season well with salt and pepper. Set aside.

4 Get a skillet/frying pan very hot. Rub your steak all over with sunflower oil. Season well with black pepper. Sprinkle salt over one side, then place, salt-side facing down, in the hot pan. Cook for 1 minute or so, season the top of the steak, then flip. Cook for another minute on the other side, then repeat the flip twice. Remove from the pan and leave to rest for a few minutes. Cut into thick slices.

5 Spread two-thirds of your potato "nachos" on a large sheet of baking parchment. Add half the peppers and onions. Add the rest of the nachos, then arrange the steak slices over the top. Finish with the remaining peppers and onions, and top the lot with the grated provolone.

6 Bake for 5 minutes to allow the cheese to melt in and around the nachos. Top with oregano and diced tomato (if using). Enjoy!

There's a trend in the food world to use verbs as nouns. Modern cookbooks are awash with grills, wraps, twists, and bakes. However, "insert" doesn't quite have the same ring to it, so we've tastefully called this delicious dish "Guinness Beer Can Chicken." Thought to have originated from American tailgate parties in the late 70s, we have used stout rather than lager, so this variation on the usual creates a far richer taste and a more memorable BBQ sauce. Even if those memories are soon forgotten due to all those spare cans of Guinness.

SERVES   4–6
HOW EASY?   WITH EYES CLOSED

GUINNESS BEER CAN CHICKEN

1 top-quality free-range chicken, about 3¾ lb/1.7kg, at room temperature, leg tips removed

1 tablespoon salt

2 tablespoons freshly ground black pepper

15 fl oz/440ml can of Guinness

1¼ cups/300ml barbecue sauce

2 tablespoons dark soy sauce

2 tablespoons light soy sauce

French fries and coleslaw, to serve

1 Preheat the oven to 200°C/400°F/Gas 6. Place an oven rack on the lowest set of runners.

2 Rub your chicken all over with the salt and pepper.

3 Pour out half of your Guinness can and save for later. Place the opened can containing the remaining Guinness upright on a baking tray and carefully lower your chicken onto it, so the can goes into the cavity. Place in the preheated oven and cook for 1 hour.

4 Meanwhile, pop the barbecue sauce, remaining Guinness, and both soy sauces in a pan and heat through until nice and thick.

5 After 1 hour remove the chicken from the oven. Glaze with your sauce (saving the rest for serving), then chuck back in the oven for 15 minutes. Watch it doesn't fall over!

6 Remove and leave to rest for 20 minutes before demolishing. Serve with fries, coleslaw, and additional sauce. Enjoy!

I know what you're thinking. NO, NO, NOOOO. "Would this even taste good?" "A twist too far, I say!" "What are Twisted on about?" Well, my friends, you're wrong. Look, we just like to live life on the edge. We love lasagne and we love creamy, tomato-based, spiced gravies with our grilled chicken. We only went and did it, didn't we! Go on, live a little.

BUTTER CHICKEN LASAGNE

SERVES 4
HOW EASY? SWEATING A BIT

6–8 boneless, skinless chicken thighs, depending on size

½ cup/100g Greek yogurt (the thick, strained variety)

1 teaspoon ground cinnamon

1 inch/2.5cm piece of fresh ginger, crushed into a paste

4 fat garlic cloves, crushed into a paste

2 tablespoons smoked sweet paprika

1 teaspoon garam masala

1 tablespoon ground coriander

1 tablespoon chili powder (try to find the Kashmiri variety as it has a great color!)

salt

½ cup/115g unsalted butter, plus extra for brushing

1 onion, diced

2 hot green chilies, sliced

5 tablespoons tomato paste/purée

1¼ cups/295ml heavy/double cream

2 tablespoons runny honey, or to taste

3 tablespoons freshly chopped cilantro/coriander

juice of ½ lemon

1 cup/90g grated Cheddar cheese

18 oz/500g fresh lasagne sheets

1 Chop your chicken thighs into skewer-able pieces. Place in a large bowl with the yogurt, cinnamon, half of your ginger and garlic pastes, half the paprika, the garam masala, ground coriander, 1 teaspoon chili powder, and a good amount of salt. Stir to combine, then place in the fridge to marinate for a couple of hours.

2 Skewer all the chicken pieces and brush generously with butter. Pop under a screaming hot broiler/grill for 15–20 minutes, turning halfway through.

3 Preheat the oven to 200°C/400°F/Gas 6.

4 Meanwhile, crack on with your sauce. Melt the butter in a large non-stick sauté pan. Add the onion and cook for 15 minutes or so over a low-ish heat. You want a bit of color on them, but not too much. Add the remaining ginger and garlic pastes and the sliced green chilies, and cook off very briefly to get rid of the raw flavor. Add the remaining paprika and chili powder, then chuck in the tomato paste/purée. Cook briefly. Add the cream, honey, and some salt, and stir to combine.

5 Remove the cooked chicken from the skewers and dice up a bit—this will make the lasagne easier to build.

6 Remove a bit of sauce from the pan and save this for the top of the lasagne. Add the chicken to the pan along with the chopped cilantro/coriander and a good squeeze of lemon. Mix and check for seasoning.

7 Layer your lasagne. Pop a third of the chicken curry in a baking dish, then a third of your cheese, and now a layer of lasagne. Repeat until you have three layers. Top with the reserved sauce and finish with a layer of cheese.

8 Cover with foil and bake in the preheated oven for 40 minutes, then uncover and cook for a further 10 minutes. Destroy.

6 duck legs, at room temperature

1 tablespoon fennel seeds, ground

1 teaspoon ground cinnamon

½ tablespoon black peppercorns, ground

½ tablespoon fine salt

a large glass of apple juice

a small glass of dry sherry

6–8 soft buns, to serve

FOR THE HOISIN BARBECUE SAUCE:

1 garlic clove, crushed

1 tablespoon vegetable oil

3 tablespoons dry sherry

½ cup/120ml hoisin sauce

1 tablespoon rice vinegar

2 tablespoons tomato ketchup

1 tablespoon light soy sauce

½ teaspoon sesame oil

FOR THE SLAW:

¼ of a white cabbage, finely shredded

½ cucumber, cut into fat matchsticks

2 scallions/spring onions, finely sliced

small handful of fresh mint leaves

small handful of cilantro/coriander leaves

1 mild red chili, sliced

2 tablespoons rice vinegar

½ teaspoon sesame oil

salt

Twisted are on a mission to rescue duck from tired old take-out pancakes and those weird wraps you get in sandwich shops that look really long but are actually really small. So, please take this opportunity to forgive your duck-related sins and give the world's most misunderstood meat what it deserves. Napkins come recommended.

HOISIN BBQ PULLED DUCK BUNS

1 Preheat the oven to 200°C/400°F/Gas 6.

2 Rub the duck legs all over with the ground fennel seeds, cinnamon, pepper, and salt, then place in a large roasting tray. Pour the apple juice and sherry around the legs. Roast in the preheated oven for 20 minutes, then drop the temperature to 160°C/325°F/Gas 3 and cook for another hour. The meat should be falling off the bones. If not, cook for another 10–20 minutes. If the liquid looks low at any point, top up with a little water. Bring out and shred the meat once cool enough to handle.

3 Make your BBQ sauce. In a small saucepan, fry the garlic in the vegetable oil until sticky, then add the rest of the sauce ingredients. Add any leftover duck juices from the roasting tray. Cook down until bubbly and thick. Add to your shredded meat and toss to lightly coat.

4 Toss all the slaw ingredients together in a large bowl.

5 Pop some pulled duck and a little slaw into a soft, warmed bun. Come on!

We're all for fusion food, but we really pushed the (gravy) boat out with this one. Luckily there was no actual gravy involved here, but this recipe certainly cuts the mustard (oh dear). By combining the best snack in France with the well-known Neapolitan classic, this dish breaks down barriers, unifies nations, and leaves foodies in awe. If you love cheese more than a mouse with a thyroid problem, you should definitely make this.

CROQUE MONSIEUR CROISSANT LASAGNE

SERVES   6
HOW EASY?   WITH EYES CLOSED

6 all-butter fresh (or slightly stale!) croissants

Dijon mustard

9 thick slices of cooked ham

6 slices of Emmental cheese, plus ¾ cup/90g grated

FOR THE BÉCHAMEL SAUCE:

½ cup/115g unsalted butter

½ cup/60g all-purpose/plain flour

1¼ cups/300ml whole milk

1½ cups/150g grated Gruyère cheese

a few good gratings of nutmeg

salt and freshly ground black pepper

1 Preheat the oven to 200°C/400°F/Gas 6.

2 Make your béchamel sauce. Melt the butter in a pan and, as it begins to foam, stir through the flour. Cook for a minute over a medium heat, then gradually whisk in the milk, a little at a time, until smooth. Turn the heat down and simmer for a few minutes until thickened, then take off the heat and stir through the Gruyère until melted. Grate in a little nutmeg, stir, and season lightly. Pop a lid on and set aside.

3 Slice your croissants in half. Swipe each bottom half with some mustard and top with a slice of ham and then a slice of Emmental. Top with the other half of the croissants. Place half the croissants in a baking dish—they want to fit snugly. Top with half the grated Emmental and the remaining three slices of ham. Now go down with another layer of croissants.

4 Pour your béchamel sauce over the croissants and top with the remaining grated Emmental.

5 Bake in the preheated oven for 20 minutes. Nice with fried eggs.

Right, we couldn't not include a mac 'n' cheese recipe. It's us, man! But with so many great twists already out there, we thought there was only one way to justify its inclusion. Twist it twice. Yeeeeerrrrrr. Put spiced sausage right inside, and put some spicy nachos on the top also. Nailed it. P.S. Try to hunt down 'nduja—it's the nicest spreadable foodstuff in the world. Period.

SERVES   6
HOW EASY?   PAINLESS

CRUNCHY SPICY SAUSAGE MAC 'N' CHEESE

4 cups/500g macaroni

3½ oz/100g 'nduja sausage, or 4 spicy cooking chorizos, meat removed from their skins

3 tablespoons/40g butter

4 tablespoons all-purpose/plain flour

2 teaspoons hot mustard powder

3¼ cups/750ml whole milk

salt and freshly ground black pepper

1 cup/80g grated Parmesan cheese, plus ½ cup/40g for topping

4 cups/300g grated Cheddar cheese, plus ½ cup/50g for topping

1 ball of mozzarella cheese

a couple of handfuls of crushed spicy nachos

1 Preheat the oven to 200°C/400°F/Gas 6.

2 Cook your macaroni in plenty of salted water until al dente (slightly under is good).

3 Meanwhile, fry off your 'nduja or chorizo meat in a pan over a low heat. Set aside a little of the cooked meat to top the dish. Add the butter to the pan, then shake in the flour and stir to create a meaty roux. Chuck in your mustard powder. Add your milk to this (as you would for a normal roux, whisking as you go). You should have a bright orange sauce. Cook for 20 minutes over a gentle heat to thicken slightly, stirring occasionally. Season with salt and lots of black pepper. Add your Parmesan and Cheddar to the sauce in batches, stirring until all incorporated.

4 Drain the pasta and add to your sauce. Stir through to combine and transfer the lot to a baking dish. Rip the mozzarella over the top, along with the remaining sausage meat and another generous grating of Parmesan and Cheddar. Cover in crushed nachos.

5 Cover with foil and bake in the preheated oven for 35 minutes, then unwrap and cook for a final 10 minutes. Destroy.

On one magical day in June 1889, pizza first came to be. Since then, pizza has become an Italian treasure, a household favorite, and sometimes a shoulder to cry on (guilty). From deep pan to traditionally thin, farmhouse to pepperoni, everyone has their own idea of what makes a pizza great. We think it's fair to say, pizza is a star. So why not make it look like one?

SERVES   4
HOW EASY?   PAINLESS

FOR THE DOUGH:

4¼ cups/600g strong bread flour

1½ tablespoons sugar

1 tablespoon fine salt

1½ cups/350ml lukewarm water

2 teaspoons instant yeast

2 tablespoons olive oil, plus extra for drizzling

FOR THE TOPPING:

½ cup/120ml pizza sauce, for the base

1 cup/115g mozzarella cheese, torn into small pieces

a few fresh basil leaves

1 egg white, beaten, for sealing

6 slices of smoked streaky bacon

barbecue sauce, for glazing

pizza toppings of your choice (such as sliced chorizo sausage or pepperoni)

PIZZA STAR

1 To make the dough, pop the flour in the bowl of a food processor. Add the sugar and salt and pulse to distribute. Pour in the water, then add the yeast and oil. Start the motor and run for about 20 seconds—the mixture should come together into a large, slightly sticky mass.

2 Tip the mix out onto a floured surface and knead for 5 minutes or so until you have a pretty smooth ball. Place in an oiled bowl, rub over with a little oil, cover with plastic wrap, and leave somewhere warm-ish to prove for 1 hour.

3 Preheat the oven to 240°C/475°F/Gas 9.

4 Knock back the dough and shape into a circle about 16 inches/40cm in diameter and ¼ inch/5mm thick on a floured surface. Transfer to a baking tray lined with baking parchment. Using a pizza cutter, make three cuts across the center of the dough (don't cut all the way to the outer edge of the pizza). This creates a star shape, giving you six triangles of dough.

5 Spread the pizza sauce over the base, leaving a decent circle of dough in the center untouched (where your cuts are). Add mozzarella and basil leaves to the sauced area of the pizza.

6 Brush the cut area with beaten egg white, then grab one of the triangles from the center and wrap it over the corresponding outer edge of the pizza—you may need to lift up the outer edge toward the triangle so they meet. Continue until you have completed the pizza star.

7 Wrap the slices of bacon around the joining areas. Brush the bacon with barbecue sauce and skewer with a toothpick. Add your chosen toppings to the "exposed" areas of the pizza and drizzle with a little oil.

8 Bake in the preheated oven for 15–20 minutes, then serve with French fries and salad. Enjoy!

SWEET

Bologna, 1973. Giuseppe Conte, an artisan purveyor of fine Italian salami, is mixing pork with fat, herbs, and pepper, ready to be cased and shaped into one of his prized sausages. Suddenly a plume of dark brown smoke clouds the room. Giuseppe coughs, splutters, then licks his lips. "Chocolate?!". A bag of cocoa powder had fallen from a shelf high above the mixing bowl and landed square in the mix. Throwing caution to the wind, curious as to whether he may have discovered a potentially wondrous flavor combination, Giuseppe completed the salami and sold it from his stall at the Mercato. Everyone hated it.

This story isn't true, but the recipe below is every bit as real as our imagination, and is meat-free! We chucked in Snickers because they're great, but you can substitute them for your favorite chocolate bar if you want. Enjoy, guys!

SERVES   8
HOW EASY?   PAINLESS

SNICKERS SALAMI

7 oz/200g dark cooking chocolate, broken into pieces

½ cup/100g unsalted butter

2 egg yolks

½ cup/120ml milk

2 tablespoons cocoa powder

3½ oz/100g graham crackers/ digestive biscuits, each broken into 3 or 4 pieces

½ cup/50g dried cranberries

5½ oz/150g Snickers chocolate bars, chopped into ½ inch/1cm slices

confectioner's/icing sugar, for dusting

1 Melt your chocolate and butter together in a glass bowl placed over a pan of simmering water. Remove and allow to cool slightly (for the next stage, ensure the mixture is not hot or it will cook the egg yolks). When just warm to the touch, add the yolks one by one and stir to combine.

2 In a small saucepan, heat the milk and cocoa together until it has thickened— dragging your finger through the mixture on the back of a spoon should leave a clean line. Leave to cool.

3 Add your crackers/biscuits, cranberries, and Snickers to the chocolate mix, then add the cocoa mixture. Stir gently to combine, but try not to break up the crackers too much. Cover and refrigerate for an hour or two.

4 Once the mixture is firm, empty out onto a large piece of plastic wrap. Shape the mix into a rough log with your hands. Wrap with the plastic wrap and continue to shape. A few bobbles and lumpy bits are just fine. Pop back into the fridge for another half hour or so.

5 Bring out, unwrap, and rub all over with confectioner's/icing sugar to give it that veritable salami look. Wrap in string for additional authenticity! Slice. Great with an espresso or two.

Right, say goodbye to boring old blueberry muffins. This recipe takes deliciousness to another level by taking two of our favorite indulgences and combining them to make simply mouth-watering, chocolate marshmallow-ey wonder. This is like no muffin you've seen before. It is best eaten while the oozing marshmallow topping is still warm. This one will 100% leave you wanting s'more (sorry).

S'MORES MUFFIN CHEESECAKES

MAKES 12
HOW EASY? PAINLESS

2 cups/200g graham crackers/ digestive biscuits, bashed into crumbs

½ cup/100g unsalted butter, melted

2 cups/400g cream cheese

2 tablespoons confectioner's/icing sugar

1 teaspoon vanilla essence

6 cups/200g big white marshmallows, melted in the microwave for 30 seconds

7 oz/200g good-quality semi-sweet/dark chocolate, broken into pieces

1¼ cups/300ml heavy/double cream

5 cups/200g mini white marshmallows

1 Fill a 12-hole, 1¼ inch/3cm deep muffin pan with paper liners.

2 Tip the crumbs into a bowl and mix in the melted butter. Place a dessertspoon of the buttery crumbs into each paper muffin liner, flatten with a teaspoon, and pop in the freezer for 10 minutes or so.

3 Using an electric whisk, whip together the cream cheese, sugar, and vanilla essence. Fold through the melted big mallows. Spoon a heaped dessertspoon of this on top of each chilled base. Pop in the fridge for 30 minutes.

4 Place the broken chocolate in a bowl. Heat the cream in a pan until almost simmering, then pour over the chocolate. Leave to sit for 5 minutes, then stir to make a thick ganache-y mix. Pop a spoonful of this on top of the chilled cream cheese mixture. Chill for 20 minutes.

5 Top with mini marshmallows, then place under a preheated broiler/grill for 1 minute (alternatively, use a cook's blowtorch). Watch the cheesecakes closely to make sure they don't burn. Leave to cool slightly, then dig in.

Ladies and gentlemen, please prepare yourselves for the simplest, most crowd-pleasing dessert you'll ever eat. The whole shebang involves just three ingredients that you'll almost definitely already have in your storecupboard, meaning there's absolutely no excuse not to take this book and go and whip up a batch immediately.

MAKES 12
HOW EASY? WITH EYES CLOSED

PEANUT BUTTER JELLY CUPS

18oz/500g semi-sweet/dark chocolate
½ cup/150g raspberry preserve/ jam
¾ cup/175g smooth peanut butter

1 Melt your chocolate either in a microwave or in a heatproof bowl over a pan of simmering water, then allow to cool slightly.

2 Spoon a heaped tablespoon of melted chocolate into a paper muffin case, then place another empty case directly on top of the filled one. Gently press down on the top paper case to push the chocolate up the sides of lower paper case. Pinch the sides of the paper to encourage the chocolate all the way to the top as best you can (don't worry if it's not perfect—you will be filling in the gaps later).

3 Freeze for 15 minutes, then remove the top paper case from the lower to reveal your chocolate cup.

4 Place a heaped teaspoon of raspberry preserve in each chocolate cup, then place a heaped teaspoon of peanut butter on top. It should come up to just under the top of the cup. Smooth out slightly, then pop back in the freezer for 10 minutes.

5 Cover the top with more melted chocolate to seal in the filling, then refrigerate until you are ready to eat. Serve at room temperature. Awesome.

Sometimes, a dish comes along that is so simple, and so delicious, that you wonder why you've never thought of it before. This is one such dish. Coconut and avocado replace dairy, proving that vegans might be having some fun after all. Serving this to your fussy friends is guaranteed to put you in their good books, something they'll almost certainly thank you for with a gluten-free, nut-free, fun-free feast in the very near future. Lucky you!

SERVES 4
HOW EASY? WITH EYES CLOSED

VEGAN AVOCADO ICE CREAM

1¾ cups/400ml coconut cream
6 large, ripe haas avocados
juice of ½ lemon
seeds from ½ vanilla pod
½ cup/60ml agave syrup,
  or to taste

1 Pop the coconut cream in the fridge overnight.

2 Remove all of the flesh from the avocados and place in the bowl of a food processor along with the lemon juice, vanilla seeds, and agave syrup. Whizz to a super smooth, pale green cream.

3 Whip the cold coconut cream in a bowl with a hand blender until you have light, soft peaks.

4 Fold the avocado mixture through the coconut cream, or vice versa. Transfer the mix to a container and cover tightly with plastic wrap (to avoid freezer burn). Freeze for at least 4 hours to set. Get yer mates round!

INDEX

ACKNOWLEDGMENTS

To everyone at JC both past and present, thank you. Your ridiculous (and rarely feasible) food ideas, insatiable appetites, and words of encouragement have spurred us on at every turn. Thanks Joe for the help with the writing and editing and Josie for some legit intros. To Chris for always responding to all video- and jelly-related enquiries with aplomb. To Mel and Molly for the shares. To Charly for the legit vids. To Mitch, Sami, and Gary for the briefs. To Greg for that one idea we never did and to Lulu and Stefan for some of the weirder ones. To Chanel for crushing it. To Lyds and Rose for the support. To Stephen for the incredible snaps. To anyone that lent their hands to a vid. To Piotr, Tawfiq, Theasby, Henry, Tassy, Hayden, Cam, Callum, Chris. P, Daisy, Dylan, Emma, George, Grace, Harry.M, Jadon, Mary, Lucy, Morgan, Olivia, Piotr, Raman, Siobhan, and Tayo. To anyone else we have forgotten. Until next time!